Ulysses S. Grant

Welsbacher, Anne   Test#: 42317

Points: 0.5   Lvl: 5.2

United States Presidents

Ulysses S. Grant

Anne Welsbacher

ABDO Publishing Company

visit us at
www.abdopub.com

Published by ABDO Publishing Company, 4940 Viking Drive, Edina, Minnesota 55435. Copyright © 2001 by Abdo Consulting Group, Inc. International copyrights reserved in all countries. No part of this book may be reproduced in any form without written permission from the publisher.

Published 2001
Printed in the United States of America.
Second printing 2002

Photo Credits: Archive, Corbis

Contributing Editors: Bob Italia, Tamara L. Britton, Kate A. Furlong

Library of Congress Cataloging-in-Publication Data

Welsbacher, Anne, 1955-
    Ulysses S. Grant / Anne Welsbacher.
      p. cm. -- (United States presidents)
    Includes index.
    Summary: Follows the life and career of the man who served as a Union general, helped the North win the Civil War, and became the eighteenth president of the United States.
      ISBN 1-56239-741-9
      1. Grant, Ulysses S. (Ulysses Simpson), 1822-1885--Juvenile literature. 2. Presidents--United States--Biography--Juvenile literature. 3. Generals--United States--Biography--Juvenile literature. 4. United States. Army--Biography--Juvenile literature. [1. Grant, Ulysses S. (Ulysses Simpson), 1822-1885. 2. Presidents. 3. Generals.] I. Title. II. Series: United States presidents (Edina, Minn.)
E672.W45   2001
973.8'2'092--dc21
   [B]   97-53069
                                           CIP
                                         AC

Contents

Ulysses S. Grant

*U*lysses S. Grant was the eighteenth president of the United States. As an army **general**, he helped the **Union** win the Civil War.

The **Republicans** chose Grant to run for president in 1868. He easily won the election. President Grant passed a law to make American **currency** more stable. He also signed the Fifteenth **Amendment** to the U.S. **Constitution**.

Grant was re-elected president in 1872. He faced problems in his second term. There were many **scandals** among his party members. During this time, the U.S. Army was badly defeated at the Battle of the Little Bighorn.

After serving two terms as president, Grant left the White House. In his final years, Grant and his family traveled all over the world. Then, he returned home and wrote his **autobiography**. But, Grant died of cancer before the book was published.

Ulysses S. Grant

Ulysses S. Grant (1822-1885)
Eighteenth President

BORN: April 27, 1822

PLACE OF BIRTH: Point Pleasant, Ohio

ANCESTRY: Scots-English

FATHER: Jesse Root Grant (1794-1873)

MOTHER: Hannah Simpson Grant (1798-1883)

WIFE: Julia Boggs Dent (1826-1902)

CHILDREN: Four: 3 boys, 1 girl

EDUCATION: Local schools; U.S. Military Academy at
                    West Point

RELIGION: Methodist

OCCUPATION: Soldier, farmer, real estate agent, customs house
                    clerk, leather store clerk

MILITARY SERVICE: Commissioned second lieutenant in Fourth U.S.
                    Infantry (1843), resigned as captain (1854); re-
                    entered army in June 1861 as a colonel, promoted
                    to brigadier general in August; became General
                    in Chief of Union Armies on March 12, 1864

POLITICAL PARTY:	Republican
OFFICES HELD:	Secretary of War (1867-1868)
AGE AT INAUGURATION:	46
YEARS SERVED:	1869-1877
VICE PRESIDENTS:	Schuyler Colfax (1869-1873) and Henry Wilson (1873-1875, died in office)
DIED:	July 23, 1885, Mt. McGregor, New York, age 63
CAUSE OF DEATH:	Throat cancer

Birthplace of Ulysses S. Grant

Young Lyss

*H*iram Ulysses Grant was born on April 27, 1822, in Point Pleasant, Ohio. Everyone called him "Lyss." When Lyss was a year old, his family moved to a farm in Georgetown, Ohio.

Lyss's father, Jesse Root Grant, was a **tanner**. He was honest and friendly. His mother, Hannah Simpson Grant, was shy, quiet, and strong. Lyss was quiet and strong like his mother and honest like his father.

Lyss was the oldest of six children. He had two brothers named Samuel Simpson and Orvil. He also had three sisters named Clara, Virginia, and Mary. His family did not have much money, but they were close and happy.

Lyss began school when he was about five years old. He attended a one-room school in Georgetown. Lyss enjoyed math. He could quickly solve math problems in his head.

By the time Lyss was eight years old, he had a job. He hauled wood with a horse and cart. Within a year, he had earned enough money to buy a horse. He trained and rode the horse for four years, until it went blind.

Lyss loved working with horses. People saw that he was good at it. Adults began to trust young Lyss with their horses. He often trained horses for farmers. And, he drove a **carriage** that carried people to and from Cincinnati.

At home, Lyss helped on the farm. He hauled wood, plowed fields, and harvested crops. He also helped his father in the tanning business.

But, Lyss did not like this work. So, his father asked him what he wanted to do. Together, they decided Lyss should go to college.

Grant's childhood home in Georgetown, Ohio

West Point

*I*n 1838, Grant attended the Presbyterian **Academy**. It was about 10 miles (16 km) from his home. Grant did not enjoy the classes. He already knew many of the lessons taught there.

Grant's father decided to send him to a better school. He got Grant **appointed** to the U.S. Military Academy at West Point, New York. Grant was not happy with this idea. He did not want to be a soldier. But, Grant's father made him go anyway.

In 1839, Grant started school at West Point. The school enrolled him as Ulysses Simpson Grant instead of Hiram Ulysses Grant. From then on, he went by Ulysses S. Grant.

As a West Point **cadet**, Grant studied math, physics, and engineering. Though he did not study hard, he did well in his classes.

West Point cadets also learned military skills. Grant and his classmates often took part in military drills. Grant was good at the drills with horses. Some of Grant's classmates thought he was the school's best horseman.

Grant graduated from West Point in June 1843. He finished in the middle of his class. After graduation, Grant was assigned to the Fourth U.S. Infantry at Jefferson **Barracks** in St. Louis, Missouri. He served as a **brevet second lieutenant**.

Second Lieutenant Grant

Soldier & Family Man

*I*n the Jefferson **Barracks**, Grant served with one of his old West Point roommates, Frederick T. Dent. Dent's family lived near the barracks. Grant was often welcomed into their home. There, he met Frederick's younger sister, Julia.

Julia and Ulysses both liked horses and often rode together. They also enjoyed reading poetry to each other and taking walks together. Soon, Julia and Ulysses had fallen in love.

The army moved Grant to Louisiana in 1844. The next year, Grant visited Julia in St. Louis. They became engaged. But, before they could get married, the army sent Grant to fight in Mexico.

The Mexican War began in 1846. The U.S. and Mexico fought over land. Mexico did not like that the U.S. had **annexed** Texas. And, the two countries disagreed about the border between Texas and Mexico.

During the war, Grant fought in many battles that led to the fall of Mexico City. He received two **promotions** for his bravery. By the end of the war, he had become a **brevet captain**.

The United States won the Mexican War in 1848. Grant returned to St. Louis. He married Julia Dent on August 22, 1848. Two years later, the Grants had their first son, Frederick. They would have three more children named Jesse, Ellen, and Ulysses, Jr.

In 1851, the army sent Grant to the Pacific Coast. He had to leave his family behind. During this time, Grant was **promoted** to **captain**. But, he missed his family and grew bored with his job. So, he quit the army in 1854 and returned to Missouri.

Back home, Grant tried to farm. But, after four years of hardships, he quit. Then, Grant started a real estate company, but it failed. So, he and his family moved to Galena, Illinois. There, he worked in his father's leather shop.

The Grant family

A Civil War Hero

*A*s the Grant family settled into their new home in Galena, the U.S. faced serious problems. The northern and southern states disagreed about states' rights. The South thought each state should have the right to allow slavery. The North wanted to end slavery in all states.

In 1860, Abraham Lincoln was elected president. He led the **Republican** party, which wanted to end slavery. After Lincoln became president, eleven southern states **seceded** from the **Union**. They formed the **Confederate States of America**.

President Lincoln

On April 12, 1861, Confederate soldiers attacked Fort Sumter in Charleston, South Carolina. This attack started the Civil War. Lincoln called for volunteer Union soldiers. Grant organized Galena's volunteers and trained them to be Union soldiers.

14

In June 1861, the governor of Illinois made Grant the **colonel** of the Seventh District Regiment. The next month, Lincoln **promoted** Grant to **brigadier general** of volunteers. In August, he received command of all the troops of southeast Missouri.

In 1862, Grant's troops successfully attacked Fort Donelson in Tennessee. The **Confederate** army's General Buckner asked Grant for terms of surrender. Grant said, "No terms but **unconditional surrender**." The Confederate troops surrendered to Grant on February 16, 1862. It was the **Union's** first Civil War victory.

Grant's success at Fort Donelson made him famous. He was promoted to **major general** of volunteers.

In April 1862, Confederate soldiers attacked Grant and his troops at Shiloh in Tennessee. More than 1,700 Union soldiers died, more than 8,000 were wounded, and nearly 1,000 were missing. Though Grant won the battle, all the casualties hurt his **reputation**.

At Vicksburg, Mississippi, Grant and his soldiers fought the **Confederate** troops through the winter of 1862 and spring of 1863. Grant's troops finally defeated the Confederate soldiers on July 4, 1863. Grant's victory at Vicksburg badly weakened the Confederacy.

In November 1863, Grant and his troops went to Chattanooga, Tennessee. They rescued **Union** soldiers surrounded by the Confederates. This victory brought Grant more fame.

In 1864, Grant was **promoted** to **lieutenant general** of all the Union armies. He created bold attack plans to defeat the Confederate army, which was led by General Robert E. Lee.

In 1864, Grant led Union troops into many bloody battles. More than 17,000 Union soldiers died at the Battle of the Wilderness in May. The next month 6,000 more Union soldiers died at Cold Harbor. People started calling General Grant "Grant the Butcher."

Civil War battle map

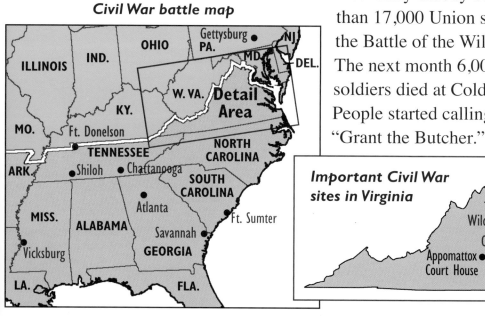

Important Civil War sites in Virginia

General Robert E. Lee

But, Grant continued with his plans. In June 1864, he led **Union** soldiers to Petersburg, Virginia. The fighting in Petersburg lasted nearly a year. During this time, other Union troops attacked Georgia and the valley of Virginia.

The Union's attacks cornered the **Confederate** army. General Lee knew more fighting would be useless. So, on April 9, 1865, Lee surrendered to Grant at Appomattox Court House, Virginia.

After the war, President Lincoln planned to bring the North and South together peacefully. But, Lincoln was **assassinated** on April 14, 1865. Vice President Andrew Johnson became the new president.

Johnson brought the Southern states back into the Union. This is called Reconstruction. Johnson asked Grant to tour the South and report on the damaged cities. Under Johnson, Grant also served briefly as **Secretary of War**.

The **Republicans** admired Grant's work in the Civil War and the national government. So, they **nominated** him for president. He beat his opponent, Horatio Seymour, and became America's eighteenth president in 1868.

The Making of the Eighteenth United States President

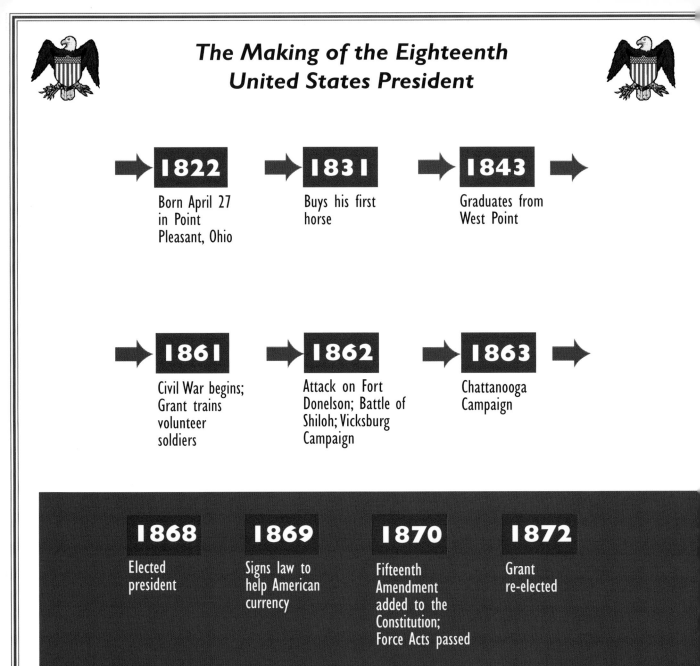

1822
Born April 27 in Point Pleasant, Ohio

1831
Buys his first horse

1843
Graduates from West Point

1861
Civil War begins; Grant trains volunteer soldiers

1862
Attack on Fort Donelson; Battle of Shiloh; Vicksburg Campaign

1863
Chattanooga Campaign

1868
Elected president

1869
Signs law to help American currency

1870
Fifteenth Amendment added to the Constitution; Force Acts passed

1872
Grant re-elected

PRESIDENTIAL YEARS

Ulysses S. Grant

"I ask patient forbearance one toward another throughout the land, and a determined effort on the part of every citizen to do his share toward cementing a happy union . . ."

1846
Fights in the Mexican War

1848
Marries Julia Dent on August 22

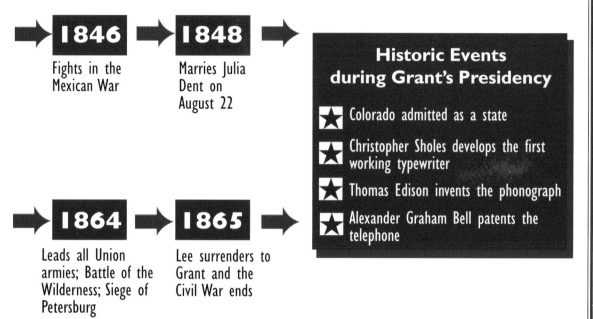

Historic Events during Grant's Presidency

★ Colorado admitted as a state

★ Christopher Sholes develops the first working typewriter

★ Thomas Edison invents the phonograph

★ Alexander Graham Bell patents the telephone

1864
Leads all Union armies; Battle of the Wilderness; Siege of Petersburg

1865
Lee surrenders to Grant and the Civil War ends

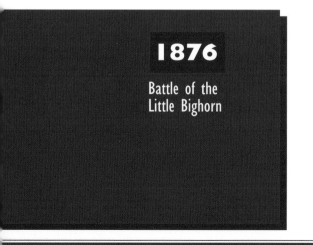

1876
Battle of the Little Bighorn

1877
Leaves the White House and tours the world

1885
Finishes his book; dies on July 23

President Grant

*P*resident Ulysses S. Grant took office on March 4, 1869. He was 46 years old. At the time, he was the youngest president in U.S. history.

Grant signed his first law on March 18, 1869. The law promised to replace greenbacks with gold. The Union used greenbacks instead of gold during the Civil War. But, the value of this paper money could fall. Gold's value was much steadier. It was a better **currency**.

Two **financiers**, Jay Gould and James Fisk, wanted to control America's gold supply and drive up its price. They tried to use Grant to reach their goal. Grant stopped them. But, the **scandal** still hurt the U.S. **economy**.

President Grant helped pass the Fifteenth **Amendment** in 1870. It gave freed slaves the right to vote. Grant also passed the Force Acts. These laws protected the rights of freed slaves.

President Grant wanted to increase America's territory. He tried to **annex** present-day Dominican Republic. But, **Congress** voted against it.

Crowds gather on March 4, 1869, to watch
Ulysses S. Grant take the oath of office.

Grant was popular with the American people. The **Republicans re-nominated** him for president in 1872. He easily beat the **Democrat's** candidate, Horace Greeley.

Grant's second term was difficult. Many of the people he trusted took part in **scandals**. His personal secretary, Orville E. Babcock, was involved in the **Whiskey Ring**. His **Secretary of War**, William W. Belknap, was **impeached** for taking bribes. And, Republican leaders formed a company to steal money from the Union Pacific Railroad. Though many of these people were **prosecuted**, Grant's **reputation** suffered.

Grant faced other problems, too. **Congress** wanted to open Native American lands in the west to white settlers. They wanted to put Native Americans on reservations. Many Native Americans fought back.

In 1876, the Battle of the Little Bighorn took place in Montana Territory. **Lieutenant Colonel** George Custer led troops against the Sioux and Cheyenne. Sioux and Cheyenne warriors killed Custer and hundreds of his soldiers. Grant was critical of Custer's attack. He called this battle "wholly unnecessary."

Americans began to think Grant was a poor leader. But, some **Republicans** wanted him to run for a third term. Grant did not win the **nomination**. He and his family left the White House in 1877.

The United States during Grant's presidency

Existing States

New States

Existing Territories

The Seven "Hats" of the U.S. President

To be president, a person must have lived in the country for at least 14 years, must be a U.S. citizen born in America, and must be at least 35 years old.

A president is elected or re-elected every four years.

Chief of State
- Performs official duties
- Stands as a symbol of the United States

Chief Diplomat
- Oversees relations with other countries
- Writes treaties
- Grants recognition to new governments

Chief Executive
- Oversees government programs
- Manages government workers

Commander-in-Chief
- Constructs military plans
- Maintains control of armed forces

Chief Legislator
- Proposes laws
- Reports to Congress

Chief Politician
- Leads political party
- Supports its candidates

Chief Jurist
- Appoints federal judges
- Enforces court rulings

If a president dies in office, the vice president becomes president.

A president can serve only two terms. Each term lasts four years. When Grant was president, this law did not exist.

As president, Ulysses S. Grant had seven jobs.

The Three Branches of the U.S. Government

Congress is in the Capitol Building in Washington, D.C. It can pass laws and stop the president's veto. Congress can also change the Constitution to stop the president's plans or Supreme Court rulings.

The president lives in the White House in Washington, D.C. He or she can stop (veto) laws passed by Congress, and propose new laws. The president can also choose Supreme Court judges.

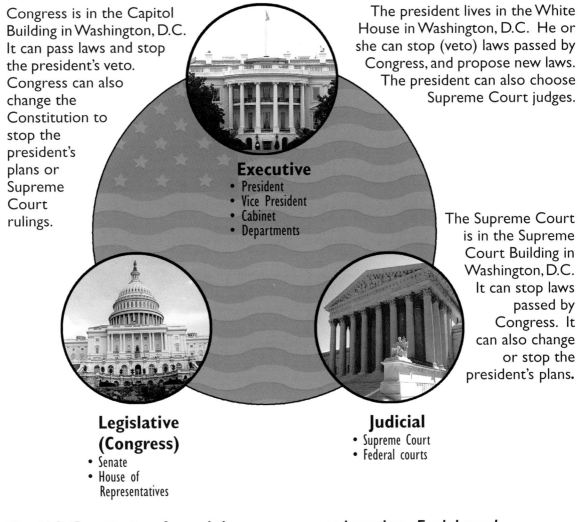

Executive
• President
• Vice President
• Cabinet
• Departments

The Supreme Court is in the Supreme Court Building in Washington, D.C. It can stop laws passed by Congress. It can also change or stop the president's plans.

Legislative (Congress)
• Senate
• House of Representatives

Judicial
• Supreme Court
• Federal courts

The U.S. Constitution formed three government branches. Each branch has power over the others. So, no single group or person can control the country. The Constitution calls this "separation of powers."

Around the World

*T*wo months after leaving the White House, Grant and his family took a trip around the world. Everywhere they went, people cheered Grant as the leader who kept America together.

The Grants spent a year and a half in Europe. Then they moved on to Africa. Grant liked visiting Egypt's ancient monuments, such as the Sphinx. Next, the Grants traveled to the Middle East and India. Then, it was on to Asia.

The Grants returned to the U.S. after two years. He thought about running for a third term as president. But, he did not have enough support to be **nominated**. Grant's political career was over.

Grant and his family had little money after their travels. He had to sell his army swords to earn extra money. Then, he became a partner in an investment firm. The business failed, and the Grants went broke.

Grant shortly before his death

While Grant searched for ways to provide for his family, he found out he had throat cancer. He wanted his family to have enough money after he died. Famous writer Mark Twain offered Grant much money for Grant's **autobiography**. Grant agreed to write it.

Though ill, Grant worked hard to write a great book. He finished it shortly before he died on July 23, 1885. Grant was 63 years old.

Grant's death saddened the country. Thousands turned out for his funeral procession in New York City. Grant is buried in a **tomb** overlooking the Hudson River. Grant's Tomb has become one of America's great national monuments.

Grant's book, *Personal Memoirs*, was published after his death. It became a best-seller. It made enough money to support Grant's family for the rest of their lives.

Grant's Tomb

Fast Facts

- While Grant served in the Civil War, his favorite breakfast was a cucumber soaked in vinegar.

- Grant's thirteen-year-old son Frederick fought alongside him at Vicksburg during the Civil War.

- Although Grant was a war hero who had seen many battles, he grew queasy at the sight of undercooked meat.

- The coldest inauguration day was in 1873, when Grant was sworn in as president. The temperature dipped to 4°F (-16°C).

- President Grant was arrested in Washington, D.C., for driving his horse and **carriage** too fast.

- The salary of the president doubled from $25,000 to $50,000 during Grant's time in office.

Grant with his son Frederick

Glossary

academy - a school that provides training in a special field, such as the military.

Amendment - a change to the Constitution of the United States.

annex - to add land to a nation.

appoint - to officially name someone for a position.

assassinate - to murder a very important person.

autobiography - the story of a person's life that is written by himself or herself.

barracks - buildings that house soldiers.

brevet - a military title given to an officer who has a higher rank than which he or she is paid for.

brigadier general - an officer that ranks above colonel and below major general. He or she has one star.

cadet - a student in a military academy.

captain - a military rank above a first lieutenant and below a major.

carriage - a wheeled vehicle, usually pulled by horses, that is used to carry people.

colonel - a military rank above lieutenant colonel and below brigadier general.

Confederate States of America - the country formed by the states of South Carolina, Georgia, Florida, Alabama, Louisiana, Mississippi, Texas, Virginia, Tennessee, Arkansas, and North Carolina that left the Union between 1860 and 1861. It is also called the Confederacy.

Congress - the lawmaking body of the U.S. It is made up of the Senate and the House of Representatives.

Constitution - the laws that govern the United States.

currency - the money that is used in a country.

Democrat - a political party. When Grant was president, they supported farmers and landowners.

economy - the way a country uses its money, goods, and natural resources.

financier - a person skilled in financial matters, such as a banker.

general - a military officer of the highest rank.

impeach - to have a trial to see if a person should be removed from office.

lieutenant colonel - an army rank above major and below colonel.

lieutenant general - an officer that ranks above major general and below general. He or she has three stars.

major general - an officer that ranks above brigadier general and below lieutenant general. He or she has two stars.

nominate - to propose a person for an office or honor.

promotion - an advancement in rank.

prosecute - to bring before a court of law.

Republican - a political party. When Grant was president, they supported business and strong government.

reputation - what people think and say about another person.

scandal - something that shocks people and disgraces those connected with it.

secede - to break away from a group.

second lieutenant - a military officer of the lowest rank.

Secretary of War - an advisor to the president who handles the nation's defense.

tanner - a person whose business is tanning hides.

tomb - a large chamber where a person is buried.

unconditional surrender - to give up everything.

Union - the states that remained in the U.S. during the Civil War.

Whiskey Ring - a scandal that broke in 1875 when Americans learned that some government workers had stolen tax money that came from the sale of whiskey.

Internet Sites

The Presidents of the United States of America
http://www.whitehouse.gov/WH/glimpse/presidents/html/presidents.html
Part of the White House Web site.

Ulysses S. Grant Association
http://www.lib.siu.edu/projects/usgrant/usgrant.html
Sponsored by the Ulysses S. Grant Association.

These sites are subject to change. Go to your favorite search engine and type in "United States Presidents" for more sites.

Index